GIANT CHILDREN

POEMS BY
BROD BAGERT
PICTURES BY
TEDD ARNOLD

SCHOLASTIC INC.

New York Toronto London Auckland Sydney
Mexico City New Delhi Hong Kong Buenos Aires

To my giant niece, Alexandra, and
my giant nephew, Christopher
—*B.B.*

For John and his big guy, Erik
—*T. A.*

ISBN 0-439-62352-9

Text copyright © 2002 by Brod Bagert.
Illustrations copyright © 2002 by Tedd Arnold. All rights reserved.
Published by Scholastic Inc., 557 Broadway, New York, NY 10012,
by arrangement with Dial Books for Young Readers, a member of
Penguin Group (USA) Inc. SCHOLASTIC and associated logos
are trademarks and/or registered trademarks of Scholastic Inc.

12 11 10 9 8 7 6 5 4 3 2 1   4 5 6 7 8 9/0

Printed in the U.S.A.   40

First Scholastic printing, January 2004

Designed by Nancy R. Leo-Kelly
Text set in Bembo
The artwork was prepared with color pencils and watercolor washes.

Giant Children

Psst! Listen very closely,
There's something you should know.
It's all about a giant school
Where giant children go.

Pages turn at giant speed
As giant children learn to read.
And giant brains are really quick
When working on arithmetic.

They pound the beat on giant drums
And finger paint with giant thumbs,

Sing giant songs with giant lips
And boogie-dance with giant hips.

Giant shoes on giant feet
And giant giggles when they meet.
I watch them hour after hour,
Giant kids with giant power.

I'm just the classroom hamster
But I promise you it's true—
This is the school where giants go,
And the giant kids are YOU.

Heart Stopper

I'm standing on the stage,
The play's about to start,
And the only sound I hear
Is the pounding of my heart.

It was everything I wanted—
My fantasy . . . my goal.
So I tried out for this play
And I got the leading role.

I learned my lines, I practiced,
I came so very far,
I dreamed about this moment—
I was going to be the STAR!

So here I am on stage,
And the play's about to start.
My life was so much simpler
Before I got this part.

Pretty Ribbon

I went for a walk by Cypress Lake,
And halfway around I spotted a snake.

A ribbon snake, pretty as could be,
The prettiest snake you'll ever see.

I put that snake in a paper sack,
Then turned around and started back.

I'm a sweet little brother and I always share,
And now I have a ribbon for my sister's hair.

Jaws

When the turtle bit my brother,
He made an awful sound.
He ran around the house,
He fell screaming to the ground.

So I whispered to the turtle,
"I'd like to be your friend.
Especially if you promise me
You'll bite my brother again."

Giddyup!

"That horsey is so big," I said,
"And I'm so very small.
Please don't put me up there, Mom,
I'm scared that I might fall."

But she sat me in the saddle
With a reassuring grin,
And when I whispered, "Giddyup . . ."
He took off like the wind.

He ran through a forest
Full of branches and trees,
So I lowered my head
And squeezed with my knees.

I said to myself,
"It's time to be bold!
Somehow I've got
To take over control."

I was gone three days,
Mom thought I was lost.
But it took me that long
To show him who's boss.

I can't believe I was so afraid,
Afraid that I might fail.
But now I wonder—yes, I do—
Do you think I could saddle a whale?

Stinky Boys

I hold my baby brother,
All powdered, sweet, and pink.
But when he makes a funny face,
His diaper starts to stink.

And that's when I remember
The baby brother rule:
Someday he's going to grow up
Like those stinky boys at school.

Booger Love

I love this little booger,
All shiny green and black.
You can hold it for a minute,
But I want my booger back.

It stays right where I put it,
It sure knows how to stick.
And if it gets too dry . . . ?
It just needs a little lick.

I can hold it on my finger,
I can flick it in the air,
I can stick it underneath a desk,
Or underneath a chair.

I can make a ball and roll it
Just to see which way it goes.
I love this booger anywhere . . .
Except inside my nose.

There's a Goblin in My Throat

There's a goblin in my throat
And he's such a nasty goat—
He always wants his way
With the words I try to say:

If I try to say "clown,"
He changes it to "frown."
If I try to say "daisy,"
He changes it to "lazy."
If I try to say "wink,"
He changes it to "stink."

It's very hard to be nice
With a goblin in your throat.
But still
I lov-vv . . . hate!

Because life is so
beautif-ff-ff . . . ugly!

And you're sweet as
sug-gg-gg-gg . . . salt!

You see?
These terrrible things I say
Are really not my fault.

Yummy Clothes

When we studied Hawaii, the fiftieth state,
We were all so excited, we just couldn't wait.

And then our teacher walked into our class
Wearing a skirt that was made out of grass!

What if a cow, I began to suppose,
Came into the room and ate all her clothes?

But I'm not a cow, I'm a kid named Eddie,
So you're safe, Mrs. Jones . . .
Just don't wear spaghetti.

The Buffalo in the Library

At school, in the library,
In section eight-one-one,
I saw a big brown buffalo
Who was having lots of fun.

His nose was in a book of poems
About trees and grass and birds,
But that buffalo wasn't reading,
He was eating up the words.

I like you, Mr. Buffalo,
And I know you have to feed,
But please don't eat my poetry books.
I need those books to read.

I'll take you to the playground
And give you grass instead,
But poetry is the food I need
To feed my hungry head.

Chocolate Maniac

I love my mother,
I love my dad,
I love my brother,
Though he drives me mad.

My teacher?
She is fine and dandy.
But I really love
My chocolate candy.

I eat it when it's hot,
I eat it when it's cold,
I eat it when it's fresh,
And I eat it when it's old.

I eat it by the ounce,
I eat it by the pound,
I eat it at the table,
And I eat it off the ground.

I eat it and I eat it
Till my belly's going to pop,
Then I eat a little more—
I don't know how to stop.

I love that chocolate taste,
Oh, so gooey, sweet, and thick,
But I've eaten way too much
And I feel a little sick.

I have got to learn to stop,
I have got to take control,
I'll give chocolate up forever...
WHEN I'M 99 YEARS OLD!

Fly Food

I went up in a swing,
Up ever so high,
Then I opened my mouth
And I swallowed a fly.

I thought of fly legs,
And those sticky fly feet
That walk on the yucky things
Flies like to eat.

It's the second worse thing
That could possibly be.
It could only be worse
If the fly swallowed me.

Spaceball

Last night I had a funny dream—
My brain's a mysterious place.
I dreamed about some aliens
Who lived in outer space.

I watched them play a game
That seemed a lot like baseball.
They played with bats and floppy hats,
But the aliens called it Spaceball.

Jupiter was the pitcher's mound,
Saturn was third base,
And the little alien kid at bat
Had a serious look on his face.

"Full count, bottom of the ninth,"
I heard the announcer say.
"This batter's trying to hit the ball
Clean out of the Milky Way."

Then I saw the ball was planet Earth!
Oh, how could it possibly be?
If he hits *that* ball, it's the end of us all,
That means . . . THE END OF ME!

I heard a shout: "STRIKE THREE, YOU'RE OUT!"
And space was filled with cheers.
But the little alien batter's eyes
Filled up with alien tears.

My dreams are strange, but last night's dream
Was the strangest dream of all.
Earth was saved by an alien
Who couldn't hit the ball.

Monster Me

Lordy-lord,
My soul's at home,
It's monster-trucks
At the Cajun Dome!

I find my seat,
I wiggle and wait,
I fix my stare
On the starting gate.

And there it is,
Roaring fire,
With titan tires—
My heart's desire.

Here comes Bigfoot!
Clap your hands!
He's crushing cars
Like soda cans!

Bigfoot, Bigfoot,
Just like me.
Boss of the world
And born to be free.

Lordy-lord,
My soul's at home,
It's monster-trucks
At the Cajun Dome!

The Princess and the Dragon

Once upon a time
In a far-off distant place
There lived a lovely princess
With a pretty princess face.

She loved a handsome prince.
She had loved him all her life.
And deep inside she always knew
Someday she'd be his wife.

Their world was picture-perfect
Until that awful day
A dragon swooped down
    from the sky
And carried her away.

But this princess was no wimp;
She drove a Masserati.
She was a champion wrestler!
She had a black belt in karate!

So when that dragon growled at her,
The princess knocked him flat,
And that fire-breathing dragon
Turned into a pussycat.

She jogged back to the castle,
Got home in time for lunch,
And the prince was glad
    his princess–bride
Could really pack a punch.

Choices

Daddy agrees I need a pet,
And Mom, you know it's true,
So I made a little list
But the choice is up to you.

An elephant, a whale,
A tiger with a tail,
An eagle to soar in the air.
A horse, a donkey,
A gorilla, a monkey,
A camel, a boar, or a bear.

Or . . . a cuddly little kitten,
I'll like whatever you do.
So now you have my list
But the choice is up to you.

Dinosaur Canary

I read it in a magazine,
It's the very latest word:
They think the giant dinosaur
Was a prehistoric bird.

Now, I love my little canary,
My tiny feathered friend,
But what if I gave it too much food?
Would it get real big again?

And then what would it eat?
The problem's plain to see:
A dinosaur canary
Might decide to chomp on me!

The Scratch

I was running and I fell
And I hurt my knee.
And I got a bad scratch
And I want you to see.

What's that? You can't find it?
But it's got to be there.
It hurts me so bad,
Please search everywhere.

If you don't ever find it,
Think what I'll miss:
No place for a Band-Aid,
No need for a kiss.

A Letter to the Tooth Fairy

Dear Tooth Fairy,

I look under my pillow and what do I see?
My tooth on the bed looking back at me!

When a kid loses a tooth, the Tooth Fairy pays,
But my tooth has been waiting for three whole days.

Now listen, Tooth Fairy, this is not very funny.
Come get this tooth and leave me some money.

Sincerely,
Me

Swamp-Stomp Rock and Roll

I have heard a lot of things
(I'm almost eight years old),
But the coolest thing I ever heard
Was swamp-stomp rock and roll.

The summer sun had almost set
When we began to walk.
Grandpa said to listen,
So I tried hard not to talk.

Where the river meets the swamp
Grandpa sat me on a stump.
Big trees, like ghosts, stood all around,
And my heart began to thump.

First I heard a cricket . . .
Then there was a pair . . .
Then a thousand more joined in
And chirping filled the air.

The summer night was turning cool
With fog as thick as smoke.
An old screech owl began to hoot
And frogs began to croak.

The night was full of fireflies
Flashing blue and green.
It was the greatest light show
Human eyes have ever seen.

Gators groaned, muskrats squealed,
Fish began to flop.
My toe it started tapping
And I couldn't make it stop.

My bootie started bouncing
And my foot began to stomp.
How my body loves to boogie
To the music of the swamp!

Burning Desire

If I could have a fire truck,
I think I'd paint it red.
I'd wear a yellow jacket
And a helmet on my head.

I'd climb behind the wheel,
I'd make the siren blow,
I'd drive around the city,
I'd give them all a show.

I'd park in front of school
So the teachers all could see,
And all the other kids in school
Would wish that they were me.

The mayor would give me medals,
I'd pin them on with pride.
The president would ask me
If I'd take him for a ride.

If I could have a fire truck,
I'd have my heart's desire.
And everything would be just fine,
Until there was a fire!

Bad Words

She actually said it,
She said it in class.
It sounded so nasty,
It sounded so crass.

The children stared,
The teacher scowled,
The custodian cried,
The principal howled.

Then poor little Patti,
My very best friend,
She opened her mouth
And she said it again.

"Bad words, bad words!"
We all began to chant.
"Never! Never! Never!
Never say the words . . . I CAN'T."

Giant Hearts

Psst! Listen, little hamster,
We have something to say to YOU.
You may think we kids are giants,
But you can be one too.

Giants don't have to be real big,
Giants don't have to be tall.
What makes someone a giant
Is not their size at all.

And even when we giants get scared,
We always do our best.
We learn from our mistakes
And forget about the rest.

Life is like a play:
We all play giant parts.
And the biggest giants are the little players
Who play with giant hearts.